AR   **ATOS B.L.**   **5.7**

       ATOS Points   **0.5**

SYMBOLS of AMERICA

The Star-Spangled Banner

Debra Hess

BENCHMARK BOOKS

MARSHALL CAVENDISH
NEW YORK

Benchmark Books
Marshall Cavendish
99 White Plains Road
Tarrytown, NY 10591-9001
www.marshallcavendish.com

Library of Congress Cataloging-in-Publication Data

Hess, Debra.
  The Star Spangled Banner / by Debra Hess.
      p. cm. — (Symbols of America)
Includes bibliographical references and index.
  ISBN 0–7614–1710–9
  1. Baltimore, Battle of, Baltimore, Md., 1814—Juvenile literature. 2. United States—History—War of 1812—Flags—Juvenile literature. 3. Flags—United States—History—19th century—Juvenile literature. 4. Key Francis Scott, 1779–1843—Juvenile literature. 5. Star-spangled banner (Song)—Juvenile literature. I. Title. II. Series: Hess, Debra. Symbols of America.

E356.B2H47 2003
929.9'2'0973—dc21

                          2003004464

Cover photo: Corbis/Bettman
Back cover: North Wind Pictures

The photographs in the book are used with permission and through the courtesy of:
Corbis: Peter Turnley, title page; Reuters New Media, Inc, 4; Bettman, 15, 23, 24, 31; Paul Souders, 19; Yogi, Inc., 28; AFP, 35. *North Wind Pictures:* 7, 8, 11, 16. *Granger Collection:* 12, 20, 27, 32.

Series design by Adam Mietlowski

Printed in Italy

1 3 5 6 4 2

Contents

CHAPTER ONE

The War of 1812

Chances are if you live in the United States, you have sung or heard the national *anthem*, the "Star-Spangled Banner." The anthem is usually played at ball games, national ceremonies, or at Fourth of July celebrations.

But do you know when this song celebrating freedom became the national anthem of the United States? It all began almost two hundred years ago, when America had only fifteen states.

◀ *The Chicago Cubs stand with their hats over their hearts during the playing of the national anthem.*

In 1803 Great Britain went to war with France. The fighting went on for years. So many British sailors were killed in this war that the British began forcing sailors from American ships to fight on British warships. The United States tried to stop this from happening, but the British claimed they were only taking back their own sailors who had *deserted* years before. Since Great Britain refused to recognize America as a free country, it considered all British sailors

Did You Know?

The "Star-Spangled Banner" actually has four verses, but the first is the most widely known and sung:

Oh, say can you see, by the dawn's early light,
What so proudly we hail'd at the twilight's last gleaming?
Whose broad stripes and bright stars, through the perilous fight;
O'er the *ramparts* we watched, were so gallantly streaming?
And the rockets' red glare, the bombs bursting in air,
Gave proof through the night that our flag was
still there.
O say, does that star-spangled banner yet wave
O'er the land of the free and the home of
the brave?

The taking of American sailors by the British helped bring about the War of 1812.

6

living in America who had fought in the Revolutionary War to be deserters. America was forced into action. On June 18, 1812, the government of the United States declared war on Great Britain.

By 1814 the war was still raging. The British captured and burned Washington, D.C., on August 24, 1814. Soon after, an American named Dr. William Beanes was taken prisoner by the enemy. Dr. Beanes was a government official who was in charge of keeping state records safe.

◄ *A British and American ship do battle in the War of 1812.*

One night, Dr. Beanes had seen two drunken British soldiers near the records house. He arrested them and tried to throw them in jail. But one of the soldiers escaped and ran back to his unit, where he told the others what had happened. A group of soldiers then returned to free the jailed man and arrest Dr. Beanes. They took him to a ship and held him prisoner.

To try and free him, the U.S. government turned to a successful Baltimore lawyer and a close friend of Dr. Beanes's for help. His name was Francis Scott Key—the man who would write the "Star-Spangled Banner."

The War of 1812 was fought mostly at sea. Here parts of the USS Chesapeake *are destroyed in a battle with a British ship.* ▶

CHAPTER TWO

Francis Scott Key

Francis Scott Key was more than just a lawyer. He was a deeply religious man who was devoted to his family. He wrote poetry for his children, fought to free slaves, and worked closely with several presidents of the United States.

Although he liked poetry, Key never took it seriously. Writing poetry was his hobby. He wrote many poems in his lifetime, enough to fill a collection. *Poems of the Late Francis S. Key, Esq.* was published in 1857.

Francis Scott Key was born on August 1, 1779, to a wealthy family in western Maryland. He grew up on the family estate named Terra Rubra, which means "red earth" in Latin.

◀ *In addition to his collection of poems, Francis Scott Key also wrote a book about literature and religion.*

He attended school nearby and graduated from college at the age of seventeen. By 1805 Key had set up a law practice in Georgetown, Maryland. He had also appeared many times arguing cases before the U.S. Supreme Court.

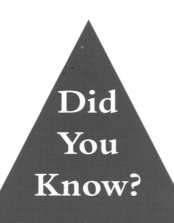

Did You Know?

- Key's brother-in-law was Roger Brooke Taney, the Supreme Court justice who gave the oath of office to President Abraham Lincoln in 1861.
- In 1934 the copy of the "Star-Spangled Banner" that Key wrote in his hotel room sold for $26,400. In 1953 the Maryland Historical Society bought it for the same price.

Terra Rubra, the birthplace of Francis Scott Key ▶

When Francis Scott Key had been told of Dr. Beanes's capture in September 1814, he was *anxious* to save his friend. He met with Colonel John Skinner, a government agent who arranged for a prisoner exchange—when a prisoner held by one side is traded for a prisoner held by the other side. Key and Skinner set sail on a small private boat to meet the Royal Navy in Chesapeake Bay.

◀ *During the War of 1812, British ships blockaded the Chesapeake River in Virginia.*

The British officers were kind to Key and Skinner and agreed to release Dr. Beanes. But the three men would have to wait. They were ordered to stay on their ship. They were kept under guard and were not allowed to return to Baltimore. On September 13, 1814, the British attacked Baltimore's Fort McHenry. From 8 miles (12.8 kilometers) away, on board the American ship, the three men watched in horror as the fort was bombed.

An aerial view of Fort McHenry today ▶

CHAPTER THREE

Bombs Bursting in Air

The British bombed Fort McHenry for twenty-five hours. One thousand five hundred shells were used. The defenders of the fort fired back, but their cannon shots could not reach the British ships. To add to their worries, during the night, British troops landed on shore and stormed the fort from the rear.

◄ *Starting on September 13, 1814, the British bombed Fort McHenry.*

From their ship, Key, Skinner, and Beanes smelled the gunpowder and heard the bombing. They thought the Americans were losing the fight. But when the bombing finally stopped, Francis Scott Key looked through the smoky air and saw an enormous American flag waving in the wind. The fort still stood! Though many American soldiers had lost their lives, the British had not been able to do much damage to the fort. When the British ships sailed in closer, the bombs from Fort McHenry flew into the air and *demolished* many of them. The ships that remained soon retreated. The sight of the flag filled Key with pride and inspired him to write a poem on the back of a letter he had started. It began, "Oh, say can you see . . ."

An inspiring sight. Francis Scott Key gazes at the American flag flying over Fort McHenry from on board the ship.

When the British *fleet* finally *withdrew*, the three men were returned to Baltimore. Key checked into a hotel and immediately set about finishing his poem. On September 14, 1814, he completed it. He showed it to his brother-in-law, who liked it so much that he took it to a printer. The poem was printed on *handbills* with the title "Defense of Fort McHenry." The author was listed as "a gentleman of Maryland."

The original flag that flew over Fort McHenry was displayed at the Boston Navy Yard until 1907. Since then, it has been kept at the Smithsonian Institution in Washington, D.C.

Did You Know?

In the summer of 1813, the commander of Fort McHenry asked for a flag so big that the British would have no trouble seeing it. Mary Young Pickersgill, a seamstress who lived in Baltimore, was hired to make the flag. She and her thirteen-year-old daughter, Caroline, cut and sewed the flag.

- Mary and Caroline used 400 yards (366 meters) of wool to make the flag.
- The finished flag measured 30 feet (9.1 m) by 42 feet (12.8 m).
- The fifteen stars on the flag measured 2 feet (0.6 m) from point to point.
- The flag was so large it had to be laid out and sewn on the floor of a local brewery.

By October the poem was being printed in newspapers across the country. Key set the poem to the music of a popular English song called "To *Anacreon* in Heaven." The composer of the song is thought to have been John Stafford Smith, an Englishman born in 1750. When the words and music were printed together, Americans fell in love with the song. It was first performed on October 19, 1814, at the Holliday Street Theatre in Baltimore. Eventually the song was renamed the "Star–Spangled Banner."

Francis Scott Key finished writing the "Star-Spangled Banner" at the Indian Queen Hotel in Baltimore in 1814. Here is a copy of the original handwritten poem. ▶

O say can you see ~~through~~ by the dawn's early light,
What so proudly we hail'd at the twilight's last gleaming,
Whose broad stripes & bright stars through the perilous fight
O'er the ramparts we watch'd, were so gallantly streaming?
And the rocket's red glare, the bomb bursting in air,
Gave proof through the night that our flag was still there,
O say does that star spangled banner yet wave
O'er the land of the free & the home of the brave?

On the shore dimly seen through the mists of the deep,
Where the foe's haughty host in dread silence reposes,
What is that which the breeze, o'er the towering steep,
As it fitfully blows, half conceals, half discloses?
Now it catches the gleam of the morning's first beam,
In full glory reflected now shines in the stream,
'Tis the star-spangled banner — O long may it wave
O'er the land of the free & the home of the brave!

And where is that band who so vauntingly swore,
That the havoc of war & the battle's confusion
A home & a Country should leave us no more?
— ~~Their blood~~
Their blood has wash'd out their foul footstep's pollution.
No refuge could save the hireling & slave
From the terror of flight or the gloom of the grave,
And the star-spangled banner in triumph doth wave
O'er the land of the free & the home of the brave.

O thus be it ever when freemen shall stand
Between their lov'd home & the war's desolation!
Blest with vict'ry & peace may the heav'n rescued land
Praise the power that hath made & preserv'd us a nation!
Then conquer we must, when our cause it is just,
And this be our motto — "In God is our trust,"
And the star-spangled banner in triumph shall wave
O'er the land of the free & the home of the brave.

After the war, Francis Scott Key became the U.S. District Attorney. He lived a few miles from the White House with his wife, Mary, and their six sons and five daughters.

On January 11, 1843, Francis Scott Key died while visiting his sister in Baltimore. He was buried in a cemetery in Maryland where an American flag flies day and night, as a reminder of the day in 1814 when he wrote the poem that would become the U.S. national anthem.

Francis Scott Key is buried in Mount Olivet Cemetery in Maryland. A monument to him stands at the grave site.

Over the years, the "Star-Spangled Banner" has become more and more popular. In the 1890s it became the official song of both the U.S. Army and the U.S. Navy. In 1916 President Woodrow Wilson ordered the song to be played at all official occasions. But it was not until 1931 that Congress decided to make the "Star-Spangled Banner" the national anthem of the United States of America. On March 3, 1931, President Herbert Hoover signed into law the bill that made it official.

President Woodrow Wilson at the World Series in 1915

▶

Today, everyone knows at least some of the words to the "Star-Spangled Banner." It has inspired generations of Americans to be proud of their country and their flag. The song is about America's survival, no matter what hardships the country may face.

◀ *Printed sheet music of the "Star-Spangled Banner" was first sold in Baltimore in 1814. Note that the word* patriotic *was accidentally spelled wrong.*

The original flag that inspired the national anthem—the one that Francis Scott Key saw flying at Fort McHenry—has been recently restored at the National Museum of American History at the Smithsonian Institution in Washington, D.C.

Despite the care it has received, the flag is very old and its fibers are weak. A special team of experts has been working on *preserving* the flag for future generations of Americans. It is an important and lasting symbol of freedom—along with the anthem it inspired.

The original flag that first inspired Francis Scott Key in 1814

Glossary

Anacreon—A Greek poet of the sixth century B.C.E.

anthem—A religious or national song.

anxious—Worried.

blockade—To prevent from entering.

demolish—To destroy.

desert—To abandon someone or something, or to run away from the army.

fleet—A group of warships under one command.

handbill—A small, printed piece of paper given out by hand.

preserve—To keep or save something from breaking down or rotting away.

ramparts—The wall surrounding a fort or castle built to protect against attack.

withdraw—To drop out or go away.

Find Out More

Books

Kent, Deborah. *The Star-Spangled Banner.* Danbury, CT: Children's Press, 1995.

Kroll, Steven. *By the Dawn's Early Light: The Story of the Star-Spangled Banner.* New York: Scholastic, 2000.

Quiri, Patricia Ryon. *The National Anthem.* Danbury, CT: Children's Press, 1998.

Spier, Peter, illus. *The Star-Spangled Banner.* New York: Yearling Books, 1992.

Web Sites

Ben's Guide to U.S. Government for Kids
http://bensguide.gpo.gov

The Smithsonian
The Star-Spangled Banner
The Flag that Inspired the National Anthem
http://web8.si.edu/nmah/htdocs/ssb-old/2_home/fs2.html

The Star-Spangled Banner
http://www.geocities.com/Athens/Troy/9087/flag/star.html

The Star-Spangled Banner
http://cincinnati.com/nie/archive/07-24-01/

Index